Hayley Helps A Friend In Need

Written By
Jenelle French

Illustrated By
Karina Yasinova

Published and written by Jenelle French

ISBN: 978-1-7356521-2-2 (Paperback)
978-1-7356521-3-9 (Hardback)

Library of Congress Control Number: 2020922272

Copyright © 2020 by Jenelle French

No part of this publication may be stored in a retrieval system or replicated, redistributed, given away, or transmitted, in any form, or by any means, electronic, mechanical, photocopying, recording, or otherwise, without prior permission of the author.

All rights reserved worldwide

www.jenellefrench.com

jenelle@jenellefrench.com

Dedicated to my amazing family.

Hi! My name is Hayley, the amazing problem solver. I can use my problem-solving skills to help others!

"Pete is a big baby!" shouted Thomas to the other kids. Pete lowered his eyes and slowly walked away from the group.
Should I ignore what was happening?
Or should I say something?
I would want somebody to say something!
"Please don't call Pete a baby.
Come on Pete, you can play with us."
I can be a problem solver and help others!

While Sophia's back was turned, I saw Sarah move her game piece to another spot. Sophia turned back around and continued playing the game without noticing the piece was moved.
Should I ignore what I saw?
Or should I say something?
I would want somebody to say something!
"Let's move her game piece to where it was before," I asked Sarah nicely.
I can be a problem solver and help others!

Mr. Baxter gave our class an assignment and told us we could pick who we wanted to work with. I overheard Lucy ask Claire if she could join them. "No, you can't be in our group," said Claire. Lucy lowered her shoulders and looked down as her lip began to quiver.

Should I ignore what I heard? Or should I say something? I would want somebody to say something!

"Hey, Lucy would you like to join our group?" I asked.

I can be a problem solver and help others!

Jacob asked if he could play basketball with some boys. "No, you can't play with us!" they shouted. Jacob's smile turned into a frown as he turned his back and walked away. Should I ignore what I heard? Or should I say something? I would want somebody to say something!
I asked Jacob, "Would you like to play with us? We're playing a fun new game!"
I can be a problem solver and help others!

I want you to be an amazing, magnificent, and exceptional problem solver too! When I see or hear something that is not right, I stop and ask myself, "Would I want somebody to help me out?"
Helping someone else makes us both feel better.

It was lunch time and I quickly tore open my sandwich, when Steve grabbed Matt's fries and hid them in his lunchbox. Should I ignore what I saw? Or should I say something? I would want somebody to say something!
"Please, give his fries back.
You wouldn't like it if somebody took your fries." I said.
I can be a problem solver and help others!

Some of my classmates were passing a ball back and forth, refusing to give it back to Macy.
"Please give me the ball back," Macy asked.
"No, you can't have it," said James.
She squeezed her fist and her face turned red.
Should I ignore what I saw? Or should I say something?
I would want somebody to say something!
"Hey, please give Macy the ball back. She can't start playing the game until she has the ball," I said.
I can be a problem solver and help others!

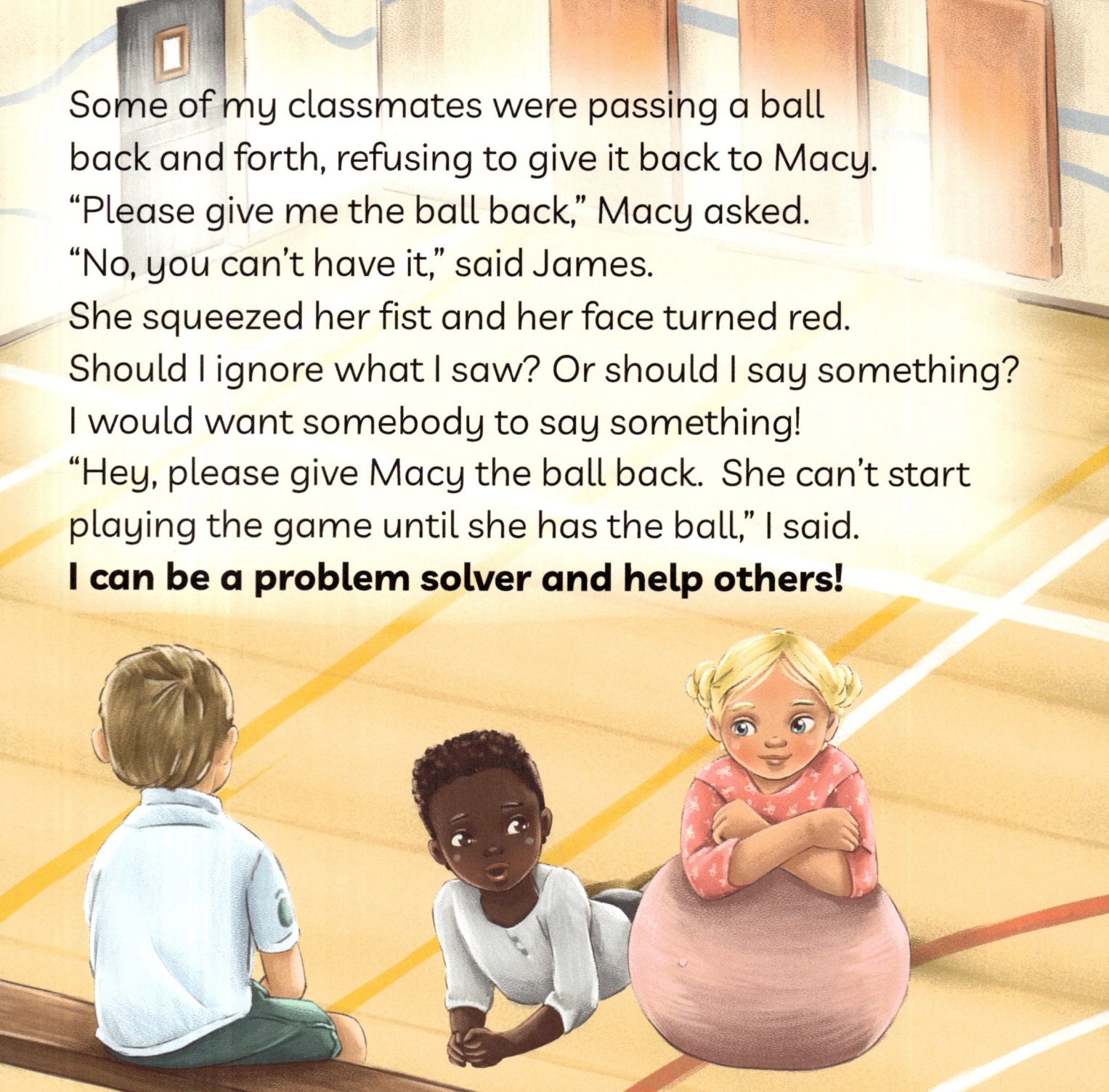

I grabbed my backpack and lunchbox and headed out the door to the bus. As I got on the bus and took my seat, a new girl sat down next to Emily. "You can't sit here. This seat is saved," said Emily. Should I ignore what I saw? Or should I say something? I would want somebody to say something! I quickly got up and walked over to the new student. "Hi, my name is Hayley! Would you like to sit with me?"

I can be a problem solver and help others!

If you see a situation where you would want somebody to help you, remember you can be an amazing problem solver too!

Dear Reader,

Throughout this story Hayley is putting herself in the other person's shoes, and chooses to help her classmates out. She is showing them empathy by inviting them to play, sit with her, and be a friend.

Empathy is putting yourself in another person's shoes and reflecting on how the other person is feeling. Children who have empathy are less likely to bully, and are generally more considerate and aware of how other people are feeling.

Take this opportunity to go back through each of the scenarios, and ask your child how the characters were feeling, and why they were feeling that way. Asking children to reflect on how other people are feeling can make a difference in helping children develop empathy for others.

In addition, ask your child, "How would you feel if someone called you a mean name, left you out of a game, etc."

I hope you and your child enjoyed reading this book as much as I have enjoyed writing it! If you found this book useful, please be sure to leave a review on Amazon. This is the best way to ensure others can find the book, and reach more children. Be sure to check out my other books in the I Can Be a Problem Solver Series, and stay up to date on more releases by visiting www.jenellefrench.com.

All my best,

Jenelle French

www.ingramcontent.com/pod-product-compliance
Lightning Source LLC
Chambersburg PA
CBHW042256100526
44589CB00002B/45